Natural Disasters

Avalanches

by

Anne Ylvisaker

Consultant:
Knox Williams, Director
Colorado Avalanche Information Center

CAPSTONE
HIGH-INTEREST
BOOKS

an imprint of Capstone Press
Mankato, Minnesota

GIFT

Capstone High-Interest Books are published by Capstone Press
151 Good Counsel Drive, P.O. Box 669, Mankato, Minnesota 56002
http://www.capstone-press.com

Library of Congress Cataloging-in-Publication Data
Ylvisaker, Anne.
    Avalanches/by Anne Ylvisaker.
    p. cm.—(Natural disasters)
    Includes bibliographical references and index.
    ISBN 0-7368-1504-X (hardcover)
    1. Avalanches—Juvenile literature. [1. Avalanches.] I.Title. II. Series:
Natural disasters (Capstone Press)
QC929.A8Y58 2003
551.3'07—dc21   2002012618

Summary: Describes how and why avalanches happen, the damage they cause, ways to avoid and survive them, and famous avalanches of the past.

Editorial Credits
Matt Doeden, editor; Karen Risch, product planning editor; Timothy Halldin, series designer; Patrick Dentinger, book designer; Jo Miller, photo researcher

Photo Credits
AP/Wide World Photos/Rudi Blaha, 40
Bruce Coleman, Inc./Arthur Greene, 10; John S. Flannery, 14; Eric Dragesco, 16; James Balog, 34; Keith Gunnar, 44
Corbis/Galen Rowell, cover, 6; Chris Rainier, 9, 36; Lloyd Cluff, 29; Bettmann, 30; Bill Ross, 33; Tim Davis, 39
Knox Williams, 22, 38
MSCUA University of Washington Libraries/Asahel Curtis, (neg#'s 17476 & 17468) 24, 26
Visuals Unlimited, 4, 47; Glenn Oliver, 13; Hugh Rose, 18; Ned Therrein, 21

1 2 3 4 5 6 08 07 06 05 04 03

Table of Contents ⟵

Chapter 1

Avalanches

In the early 1900s, a nature guide named Enos Mills often climbed the San Juan Mountains in Colorado. On one of his climbs, he reached the top of a peak just as the sun began to set. Mills decided to wait until morning to go back down. That night, snow began to fall. The snow continued until the sun rose the next morning.

Mills slowly started down the mountain. He used snow skis to take long sideways paths. Clouds covered the mountains, and he could not see far. Mills stopped for a rest at a narrow dip in the side of the mountain.

Avalanches happen when snow or ice suddenly falls down a slope.

5

Avalanches can carry millions of pounds of snow down a mountain.

Mills looked back at the mountain just as it seemed to explode toward him. Huge piles of snow rolled down the mountain. Mills knew he was watching the beginning of an avalanche.

Mills turned around, pointed his skis straight down the mountain, and skied as fast as he could, dodging trees and rocks. He saw a wide ridge in the mountain before him. Mills had no choice but to jump over it. He landed safely, but the snow crashed right behind him. He heard rocks grinding together and trees crashing to the ground.

Just as the avalanche was about to reach him, Mills saw a small crack in the rocks. He thought the crack could protect him. Mills tumbled into the crack as the snow raced past him. He had survived the avalanche.

About Avalanches

Avalanches are the natural result of gravity. As snow falls on a mountainside, it piles up in layers. Over time, the weight of these layers increases. An avalanche begins when the weight becomes too great or when an outside force loosens the heavy snow. Layers of the snow break loose and fall down the mountain. The snow can destroy everything in its path.

Avalanches happen with little warning. Many outside forces can set off an avalanche. People often start avalanches by walking or skiing on a steep slope. Vibrations from earthquakes can also start an avalanche.

People cannot stop an avalanche once it begins. Gravity pulls the snow down faster and faster. Some avalanches reach speeds of 225 miles (360 kilometers) per hour. The falling snow sets other layers of snow loose and the avalanche grows. It does not stop until the snow has nowhere left to fall.

Anyone or anything caught in the path of an avalanche will be carried by the snow or buried by it. The fast-moving snow smashes trees, destroys buildings, and buries people.

Avalanches cannot be prevented, but scientists work to predict when and where they might happen. They can tell people which areas to avoid when visiting mountains or building homes near mountains. Scientists can also set off small avalanches to avoid larger disasters later.

Scientists try to predict when and where avalanches might happen.

Chapter 2

Why Avalanches Happen

More than 1 million avalanches happen around the world every year. At least 100,000 of these avalanches take place in the United States. Avalanches can happen in any season. Most of them occur during winter when snowfall is heavy. Spring avalanches are also common. Warm air causes layers of snow to become unstable.

Snow Pack

Snow forms when water in the air turns into ice crystals. The crystals join to form snowflakes. Gravity then pulls these flakes down to the ground.

Snow forms layers on the ground. Together, these layers are called snow pack.

As snow falls, it forms layers on the ground. Some layers are made of light, loose snow. These layers often form during cold weather. Other layers are heavier and packed together more tightly. These layers often form during warmer weather.

The series of snow layers on the ground is called snow pack. When all of the layers stick together well, the risk of an avalanche is low. The risk is high when layers do not stick well to one another. Most avalanches begin where a layer of heavy snow rests on a lighter layer below.

Avalanches happen in three stages. Snow first breaks away in the starting zone. The avalanche then grows quickly. It moves down the slope, picking up more snow as it travels. During the second stage, called the track, the slope becomes less steep. The avalanche stops growing and stops gaining speed. The runout zone is the final stage. This stage happens when the avalanche reaches flat ground or hits a large object that stops it from continuing.

The runout zone is the stage where an avalanche reaches flat ground.

Slab Avalanches

The most damaging type of avalanche is a slab avalanche. A slab avalanche begins when a large layer of heavy snow breaks away from the snow underneath. This large layer, called a slab, slides down the mountain on top of the snow on the slope.

The slab of snow pushes against other slabs, which also come loose. The avalanche grows quickly. Most slabs travel between 40 and 80 miles (64 and 129 kilometers) per hour. But some slabs travel as fast as 200 miles (320 kilometers) per hour. Together, they can weigh millions of pounds.

A rush of wind called an airblast sometimes travels in front of very large slab avalanches. The airblast and the slabs often destroy trees, buildings, and anything else in their path. The falling snow can also bury people and animals alive.

Slab avalanches begin when large layers of snow, called slabs, break loose.

Loose Snow Avalanches

A loose snow avalanche happens when newly fallen snow does not stick together firmly. This powdery snow rests on a steep mountainside. An animal, the wind, or another outside force may disturb the snow. A few loose snowflakes slip down the mountain. They knock more flakes loose as they travel. Soon millions of flakes tumble down the mountain. Loose snow avalanches usually spread out in the shape of an upside-down letter "V."

Loose snow avalanches are not as destructive as slab avalanches. Loose snow is less likely to destroy objects such as trees and buildings. But these avalanches are still very dangerous to people and animals. Falling snow can bury a person in a few seconds. The weight of the snow on top of the victim can be so heavy that the person cannot move.

Loose snow avalanches often spread out in the shape of an upside-down letter "V."

Chapter 3

The Power of an Avalanche

Most avalanches go unnoticed by people. They usually happen in remote mountain areas where people do not live. But avalanches can be destructive when they happen near towns or other settlements. Small avalanches can damage buildings with wood frames. Large slab avalanches can flatten forests and crush concrete buildings.

Airblasts created by large avalanches are also destructive. They can have the same strength as some hurricane winds. People caught in an airblast can be knocked over

Avalanches can smash and bury trees. $\Leftarrow$

and buried. They can also be blown into trees or buildings.

Predicting Avalanches

Some scientists study snow and try to understand avalanches. They often work in rooms called cold labs to learn about the forces that make snow stick together. The scientists study how different types of snow react with one another.

Scientists study how snow behaves during an avalanche. A Japanese scientist used Ping-Pong balls to study this behavior. He let 300,000 balls roll down a ski slope and watched the patterns they formed while falling. These experiments help scientists understand the forces that are at work on snow during avalanches.

People also try to predict when avalanches are likely. Snow rangers and ski patrollers work in mountain areas such as ski resorts. These workers keep track of avalanche danger. They check the mountains every day for heavy snow, cracks in the snow pack, or signs of

↪ Scientists study snow to understand avalanches.

other avalanches nearby. They may close an area of a mountain or post signs that warn people of a possible avalanche.

Avalanche Control

People start some avalanches on purpose. This practice, called avalanche control, helps to prevent larger and more destructive avalanches in the future. Workers use explosives to set off avalanches in high-risk areas. Avalanche control allows workers to decide exactly when an avalanche will take place. They can make sure no people are in the area before it starts. Avalanche control also allows workers to test the snow in an area to see if more avalanches are likely.

People use a process called redirection to control where an avalanche goes. Workers place barriers such as walls and large piles of dirt and rock in the path of a likely avalanche. The barriers change the direction the snow falls. Redirection barriers often protect buildings and roads.

Workers sometimes set off explosives to start avalanches.

Chapter 4

Famous Avalanches

People do not worry about most avalanches. Even large avalanches go unnoticed when they happen in remote areas. But some avalanches hit populated areas. These disasters can kill people and cause millions of dollars in damage.

Wellington Avalanches, 1910

In late February 1910, two passenger trains ran though the Cascade Mountains near the town of Wellington, Washington. The area had received heavy snowfall that winter. Lumber companies had cut down many of the area's trees. On a slope above the railroad tracks, a small avalanche began moving down the

The first Wellington avalanche covered railroad tracks and caused trains to stop.

mountain. The avalanche came down on the train tracks, blocking the trains' way. Workers cleared the tracks. The trains then sat on sidetracks while railroad officials waited for the bad weather to improve.

Early on the morning of March 1, a thunderstorm struck the area. During the storm, another large avalanche started. It roared down the mountain and hit the trains. The force of the snow lifted both trains off the tracks and sent them falling 150 feet (46 meters) down the mountain. The disaster killed 96 people aboard the trains. Only 22 people survived.

The town of Wellington quickly became known for the disaster. Town officials changed the name of the town to "Tye" so people would not think of the avalanches. Railroad officials later built strong snow sheds over 9 miles (14 kilometers) of tracks in the area to protect trains from future avalanches.

The second Wellington avalanche swept two trains off the tracks and sent them down the mountain.

World War I Avalanches

During World War I (1914–1918), avalanches became weapons. The Austrian and Italian armies faced one another in a mountain range called the Alps. Soldiers sometimes climbed to mountaintops overlooking enemy camps. The soldiers held long ropes over areas with deep snow pack. They pulled the ropes back and forth in a sawing motion to loosen the slabs of snow. Other soldiers shot bullets into the snow to loosen it.

The avalanches caused by the soldiers usually were small. But they were still deadly. Avalanches killed between 40,000 and 80,000 soldiers over a period of three years. One Austrian officer said after the war that the mountains were more dangerous than the enemy troops.

Nevado Huascaran Avalanches

Nevado Huascaran is the tallest mountain in the South American country of Peru. In 1962,

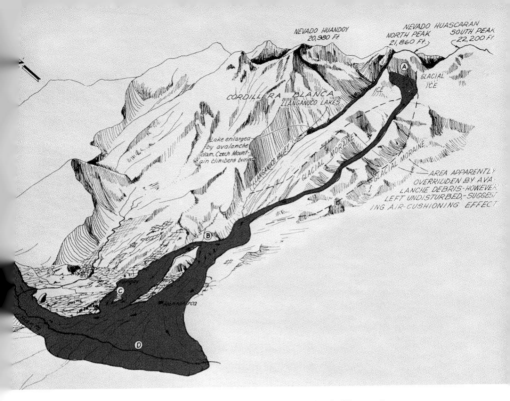

NEVADO HUANDOY
20,980 Ft

NEVADO HUASCARAN
NORTH PEAK
21,860 Ft.

SOUTH PEAK
22,200 Ft

GLACIAL
ICE

CORDILLERA BLANCA
LLANGANUCO LAKES

Lake enlarged
by avalanche
dam. Czech Mount-
ain climbers buried

GLACIAL MORAINE

GLACIAL VALLEY

LLANGANUCO VALLEY

GLACIAL MORAINE

AREA APPARENTLY
OVERRIDDEN BY AVA-
LANCHE DEBRIS-HOWEVER
LEFT UNDISTURBED,-SUGGEST
ING AIR-CUSHIONING EFFECT

This diagram shows the path of the 1970 Nevado Huascaran avalanche.

warm weather loosened a chunk of ice near the top of the mountain, starting an avalanche. On its way down the mountain, the avalanche hit a large mass of ice called a glacier. Ice broke free from the glacier, and the avalanche grew even larger.

Ice, snow, and loose rock tumbled almost 10 miles (16 kilometers) down the mountain in just seven minutes. The avalanche crushed

eight villages in the Río Santa Valley below. Some areas were buried under 80 feet (24 meters) of snow, mud, and ice. More than 3,000 people died in the disaster.

The 1962 avalanche was only the beginning for Nevado Huascaran. In 1970, a strong earthquake broke loose a huge slab of snow and rock from the face of the mountain. Scientists guess that the slab that broke loose was more than 3,000 feet (900 meters) wide and 5,000 feet (1,500 meters) long. The falling snow and rock sped down the mountain at speeds of about 200 miles (320 kilometers) per hour.

Much of the snow melted as it fell down the mountain. It mixed with dirt to create a mudslide, which flattened the town of Yungay and killed 20,000 people. The rock and snow also hit several other towns. In total, the disaster killed almost 70,000 people.

The 1962 Nevado Huascaran avalanche destroyed several villages in the Río Santa Valley.

Mount Rainier Avalanche, 1981

One of the worst mountain climbing disasters in U.S. history happened when an avalanche started on Washington's Mount Rainier on June 21, 1981. That day, 29 people were climbing the mountain. Several large chunks of ice broke loose from a glacier near the mountain's top.

Soon, a wall of snow and ice more than 30 feet (9 meters) wide was speeding down the mountain at about 130 miles (210 kilometers) per hour. Some of the chunks of ice were as large as cars. The avalanche slammed into 11 of the climbers. The force of the avalanche threw the climbers off the mountain into a deep ravine below. Their bodies were never found.

A 1981 avalanche on Mount Rainier in Washington killed 11 people.

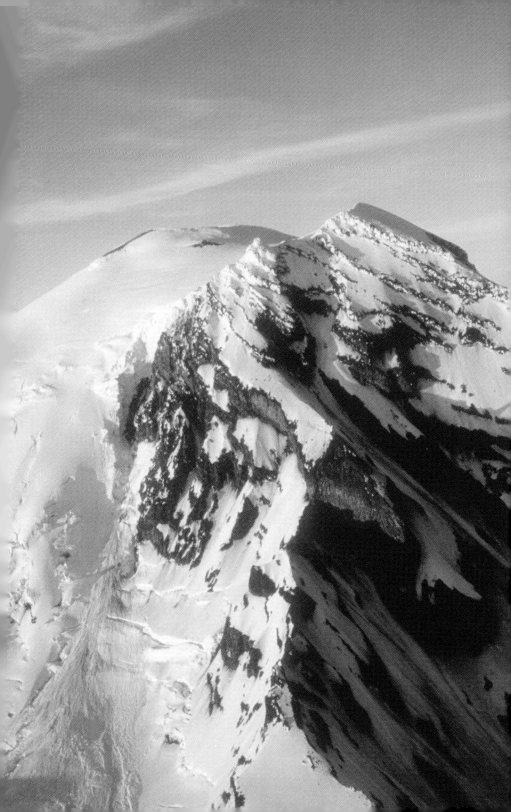

Chapter 5

Surviving an Avalanche

Avalanches are deadly and difficult to predict. They happen so quickly that people often have no time to find shelter. People can protect themselves from avalanches by paying attention to watches and warnings. They can also carry safety gear that might help them survive an avalanche.

Survival Methods

People can survive some avalanches. Many avalanche victims do not die right away. They are buried alive under many feet of snow. They are unable to move under the weight of

Most avalanches happen without warning.

the snow. They cannot even dig themselves out. People sometimes can avoid being completely buried by waving their arms in a swimming motion while being pulled by the falling snow. This action helps keep them near the surface of the snow. People are much more likely to survive an avalanche if they can keep part of their body above the snow.

Snow can harden quickly once an avalanche stops moving. Victims should use a swimming motion to try to reach the surface before the snow becomes hard. Victims who cannot pull themselves out of the snow should try to clear the snow away from their face to create breathing room. They should relax their body to save energy. They then can wait and hope rescue workers are on the way.

Equipment
People can carry equipment that will improve their chances of surviving an avalanche. The Air Bag System (ABS) is a pack that rests on a person's chest. A pull cord is attached to the

Rescue workers must find avalanche victims quickly to save them.

pack. When an avalanche breaks loose, the person pulls this cord to inflate a large air bag. The air bag helps the person float on top of the falling snow.

Skiers often wear small radio transmitters called beacons. Beacons send out a signal if the skiers are buried in an avalanche. Rescuers can track the signal to find the beacon's exact location.

Saint Bernards
In the 1100s, a monk named Bernard started an inn to take care of travelers who were lost in the Alps. Over a period of 400 years, monks from the inn saved more than 2,000 lives. Large, powerful dogs helped them find and rescue people buried in avalanches. This breed of dog was named the Saint Bernard after the monk who started the inn.

Other basic tools can help people caught in an avalanche. Skiers often carry long poles and shovels. They use these tools to rescue others buried in an avalanche. Some people also carry long, bright ropes. These ropes trail behind an avalanche victim. The bright rope helps rescuers find the victim.

Rescuers use long poles to search for victims buried in an avalanche.

German shepherds are the most commonly used avalanche rescue dogs.

Other Protection

Rescue teams often use dogs to find buried
avalanche victims. The dogs' keen senses of
smell and hearing help rescuers find people
who are buried in the snow. German shepherds

are the dog breed most commonly used for this type of rescue work.

Mountain homes, roads, and towns need protection against avalanches. Scientists can tell people which parts of town are most likely to be hit by an avalanche. Home builders can avoid those areas. Snow sheds are built over roads that are likely to be in the path of an avalanche. The sheds stop the snow before it can reach the road. Snow fences are often built above towns to slow down snow as it falls.

Safety measures cannot completely protect people from avalanches. But they can help reduce the number of lives lost due to these natural disasters.

Words to Know

airblast (AIR-blast)—a rush of wind that travels in front of some large slab avalanches

beacon (BEE-kuhn)—a small radio transmitter worn by some skiers; beacons help rescue workers find victims lost in an avalanche.

glacier (GLAY-shur)—a huge mass of slowly moving ice; glaciers often form in high mountain valleys where snow never completely melts.

gravity (GRAV-uh-tee)—a force that pulls objects toward Earth

redirection (ree-duh-REK-shuhn)—the act of building barriers that cause the direction of an avalanche to change

slab (SLAB)—a broad, flat, thick piece of something; slabs of snow break apart to begin some avalanches.

To Learn More

Aaseng, Nathan. *Avalanches.* Natural Disasters. San Diego: Lucent Books, 2002.

Drohan, Michele Ingber. *Avalanches.* Natural Disasters. New York: PowerKids Press, 1999.

Redmond, Jim. *Landslides and Avalanches.* Nature on the Rampage. Austin, Texas: Steadwell Books, 2002.

Useful Addresses ←

American Avalanche Association (AAA)
P.O. Box 2831
Pagosa Springs, CO 81147

Canadian Avalanche Centre
P.O. Box 2759
Revelstoke, BC V0E 2S0
Canada

Colorado Avalanche Information Center
325 Broadway Street, WS1
Boulder, CO 80305

Internet Sites

Do you want to learn more about avalanches?
Visit the FACT HOUND at *http://www.facthound.com*

FACT HOUND can track down many sites to help you.
All the FACT HOUND sites are hand-selected by Capstone
Press editors. FACT HOUND will fetch the best, most accurate
information to answer your questions.

IT IS EASY! IT IS FUN!
1) Go to *http://www.facthound.com*
2) Type in: 073681504X
3) Click on "FETCH IT" and FACT HOUND will put you on
the trail of several helpful links.

**You can also search by subject or book title. So, relax
and let our pal FACT HOUND do the research for you!**

Index